Will You Do Your Bit Too?

by

Tracey Özdemir

Grosvenor House
Publishing Limited

All rights reserved
Copyright © Tracey Özdemir, 2020

The right of Tracey Özdemir to be identified as the author of this
work has been asserted in accordance with Section 78
of the Copyright, Designs and Patents Act 1988

The book cover is copyright to Tracey Özdemir

This book is published by
Grosvenor House Publishing Ltd
Link House
140 The Broadway, Tolworth, Surrey, KT6 7HT.
www.grosvenorhousepublishing.co.uk

This book is sold subject to the conditions that it shall not, by way of
trade or otherwise, be lent, resold, hired out or otherwise circulated
without the author's or publisher's prior consent in any form of binding or
cover other than that in which it is published and
without a similar condition including this condition being imposed
on the subsequent purchaser.

This book is a work of fiction. Any resemblance to
people or events, past or present, is purely coincidental.

A CIP record for this book
is available from the British Library

ISBN 978-1-83975-210-0

*This book is dedicated to what we stand on,
Our Planet* 🌎

"Breakfast is ready," called Uncle Robert.

Daisy Dot and Pippi were snuggled together underneath the blankets to keep warm.

Pippi stuck her nose out from under the covers and immediately felt the cold air, making her shiver, so she quickly popped her head back underneath as it was warm and cosy there.

"Come on you two, there's some lovely hot porridge to warm you both up and give you some energy to start the day."

Daisy Dot, who still had sleep in her eyes, stretched her arms from under the covers and had a massive yawn. But the cold air made her shiver too. She reached for two hats that were on the chair by the bed. "Come on Pippi time to get up, but we are going to need our hats on today it is very cold."

"Oh, Uncle Robert, why is it so cold and, where are we?" asked Daisy Dot.

"HAHA," chuckled Uncle Robert, "it is cold because we are in the Antarctic. Now hurry up and get your winter clothes on before your porridge goes cold."

Daisy Dot and Pippi were with Uncle Robert, on his boat, for another adventure.

They loved his boat trips so much, they never knew where they would end up and were never sure what they were going to see.

The three of them were all sat around the small breakfast table enjoying their bowls of delicious porridge.

They were now feeling toasty warm and content with the delicious breakfast and with the heat coming from the little stove that the porridge pan was still sat on top of, gently bubbling away with leftovers.

"Right, we had better clear away and start the engine up and be on our way," said Uncle Robert.

"Ooooh, I hope we will see a polar bear," cried Daisy Dot as she was putting on her mittens, "I have never seen one before."

"Well keep your eyes peeled," said Uncle Robert, "they can be hard to spot with their white furry coats against the white ice. We don't one popping up and giving us a fright." This made Pippi's ears prick up. She ran and hid under the breakfast table and covered her eyes with her two front paws. This made Uncle Robert chuckle with laughter, "Don't worry Pippi everything will be alright."

Uncle Robert started the little boat engine, and off they went in the cool crystal water.

They passed lots of icebergs. As they were sailing past a very large one there was suddenly a huge splash in the water.

Daisy Dot stood there with her mouth wide open in shock; then there was another crashing noise followed by an even bigger splash.

Part of the icecap had slid down from the top of the iceberg and had crashed into the deep blue water.

Pippi began to shake with fright.

"Oh no, that's not good," said Uncle Robert.

"What's the matter Uncle Robert," asked Daisy Dot.

"The ice is melting, it is not good at all," shaking his head as he replied.

"Why is it melting?" asked Daisy Dot.

Uncle Robert lifted his cap and scratched his head and replied, "It's global warming, it means the temperature is warming up. It is not good for the animals that live here, and it is not good for the planet and it is not good for us. If everyone did a little bit at home, we could all slow the global warming process down."

"What should people do at home Uncle Robert?" asked Daisy Dot.

"Well, if we did not have as many cars on the road that would help, or changed them to electric ones. And if children went to school on the school bus, or cycled, or walked instead of being taken by car, just think how many cars would be off the road if people did that. And if people did the same going to work or when they did their daily shopping. And if we put an end to using fossil fuels too and used cleaner energy it would make a difference."

"What are fossil fuels?" asked Daisy Dot.

"Fossil fuels are coal and natural gases; we have used them for centuries but now we know that they are very bad for our planet. We can replace them with wind turbines and solar panels, a much better way to heat our homes and be kinder to our planet, if only everyone would change their ways including factories," said Uncle Robert.

"You see, humans cause these problems by using electrical appliances. We have almost seven billion people in the world, and most of them want to own a car and a house with a fridge, washing machine, and television, and air-conditioning to cool their homes and cars down, as well as central heating to keep them warm. But if people turned down the temperature of their heating that would make a huge difference, and if we washed our clothes once a week in the washing machine instead of several washes a week. Also, if we switched the television off when we weren't watching it that would help our planet.

"All the extra carbon dioxide in the atmosphere that we create from all these things traps the heat and stops it reflecting back out to space. This is how a greenhouse works, so it's known as the greenhouse effect. We keep chopping trees down, so with fewer trees to absorb carbon dioxide it means there are more CO_2 gasses in the atmosphere which then begin to warm the atmosphere up, which is not good at all," said Uncle Robert.

"What are CO_2 gasses?" asked a very curious Daisy Dot.

"That is just another name for carbon dioxide," replied Uncle Robert. "These gasses do no harm in small quantities but it is very bad for the animals and the planet; it is very bad for humans too if we keep sending huge amounts up into the atmosphere."

"Oh dear Uncle Robert, that is not good for our poor planet. Perhaps if we planted more trees that would help a little bit," said Daisy Dot.

"Yes, it certainly would Daisy Dot," said Uncle Robert, "and if we used more recycled paper, because paper is made from trees, that would make a little bit of a difference too, we can all do our bit."

They continued to sail along in the crystal waters.

"Wow," cried Daisy Dot, "look at all these pieces of floating ice."

"Yes," said Uncle Robert, "I am trying to steer the boat so we don't hit any."

Daisy Dot and Pippi went to the front of the boat, they wanted to make sure they did not hit any ice too.

Uncle Robert gently steered the boat around the chunks of ice floating on the surface of the water.

They had been sailing for some time when something caught Pippi's eye, she started to bark with excitement.

"What is it Pippi, what can you see?" asked Daisy Dot. Then Daisy Dot saw it too. "Look Uncle Robert look, look over there."

Uncle Robert looked around until he could see what they were looking at.

"Oh my," he cried. "Looks like we have found what you wanted to see Daisy Dot."

Pippi barked with delight.

They were heading towards a piece of floating ice, but this piece was a bit bigger than the rest.

And on that ice was something quite big and covered in thick white fur. It was a polar bear. But as they sailed closer, they could make out another shape, but this was much smaller.

"Mmmm, I wonder what that could be," said Uncle Robert as he scratched his head.

They sailed even closer.

"A penguin, it's a penguin," squealed Daisy Dot, who was bursting with excitement.

Pippi began barking with joy to show she was excited too.

"Mmmm, I wonder what they are doing floating on a piece of ice together," thought Uncle Robert.

As they got closer Uncle Robert shouted out, "Now what are you two doing floating around together?"

"Help. Help."

Then a squeaky "Help" could be heard too.

The boat gently sailed up to the side of the ice and just touched it.

"Well, what is happening here?" asked Uncle Robert.

"Oh, please help us," said the polar bear.

Daisy Dot and Pippi were amazed at the size of the polar bear, and his dazzling thick white coat. Daisy Dot giggled; she thought the penguin looked so tiny stood next to him.

All of a sudden, a loud splash and lots of bubbles appeared in the water at the side of the floating ice.

Then a large white head appeared. Pippi huddled close to Daisy Dot with fear.

"Oh, I am sorry, I did not mean to startle you, I am trying to push my friends back to land, but it is such hard work, I don't think I am strong enough to do it on my own."

"Who are you? And what are you?" asked Daisy Dot.

"I am Betsy, I am a beluga whale. These are my friends Chilly the polar bear, and Waddle the penguin."

"Pleased to meet you all," said Daisy Dot, "but what are you all doing out here?"

Chilly the polar bear explained, "Well I am afraid Waddle and I are in a spot of difficulty here.

"You see Waddle was going about his business. He was walking a few feet behind his family when a very loud cracking noise could be heard, then all of a sudden, the ice he was walking on broke free and started to float away.

"I just wanted to reunite the little chap with his family and save him, so I ran and jumped on to the ice to rescue him.

"But when I turned around, there was nothing I could do, we had sailed away quite fast and we are a long way from this little chap's family.

"We have ended up here, Betsy has tried with all her might to push us back to land, but the ice is far too heavy for her to push by herself."

Waddle started to cry, "So we are now stuck here," he said as he sobbed.

"Oh, now don't you cry little fellow," said Uncle Robert.

"I think we might be able to help you out.

"Now I have some rope here, if Betsy can push and if we pull with this rope, I'm sure we can get you back home safe and well."

Waddle started to walk in circles with delight, Daisy Dot thought his name suited him as he did waddle when he walked. This made her giggle to herself.

"Right, I am going to throw this rope over, do you think you can hold on to it tightly Chilly?" asked Uncle Robert.

"Oh yes, I think I can do that I am very strong," said Chilly.

"And Betsy, do you think you can push the ice with all your might?"

"Oh, I am sure I can do it with your help," said Betsy.

Uncle Robert threw the rope over, Chilly caught it and gripped it tight in his mouth with his very powerful jaw.

"Now don't let go," cried Daisy Dot.

Pippi barked as if to say hold on tight.

Uncle Robert cried out, "Now hold on, off we go."

The little boat pulled away; Chilly held on to the rope with all his strength and Betsy pushed the ice with all her might.

"Hurray, hurray," cried Daisy Dot, "it's working Uncle Robert, it's working."

Pippi ran in circles barking with happiness and delight.

The island of ice was now being pulled behind the boat like a dream.

"Well, what do we have here? said Uncle Robert.

They had been sailing along for some time when, at last, land was in sight.

"Waddle, I think I can see your family waiting for you," said Uncle Robert.

Waddle was full of relief.

As they approached land, Daisy Dot could see dozens and dozens of little figures the same shape and size as Waddle. As they got closer, she found it most amusing that they all had the same funny walk as waddle.

At last, they were home safe she thought.

The ice was pulled so close to the land that both Chilly and Waddle were able to jump off.

"Well done Betsy," cried Daisy Dot, "we could not have done this without you."

Betsy was happy she could help, but it was very hard work and had taken a lot of strength.

All the penguins rushed over to thank everyone for returning Waddle to them.

Chilly was most grateful that Uncle Robert had come along in time to save them.

Daisy Dot was so happy that everyone was safe and well.

"I am so happy you are all reunited," said Uncle Robert. "Now please stay very close to your family Waddle, we don't want you drifting off again."

"Oh, I will, I promise," said Waddle.

Both Betsy and Chilly thanked them for helping.

It was now time for them all to say their goodbyes.

"Time to go home now," said Uncle Robert, as he looked at a very cold Pippi who was shivering with the cold.

The little boat engine came to life once again.

As they sailed away Daisy Dot and Pippi waved goodbye to everyone.

The next day, Uncle Robert had prepared breakfast once again.

Daisy Dot and Pippi woke up and hungrily made their way to the little breakfast table.

But today was different, the sun was out and it felt quite hot.

"We are home, yipppppieeeee," said Daisy Dot.

Uncle Robert laughed at her excitement.

Pippi just tucked into her bowl of porridge; she was very hungry.

"Oh Uncle Robert, I am so happy Chilly and Waddle are home, and I am sure Betsy will be home swimming with her family. But I am not happy that their home is melting. Imagine if all that ice melts and turns to water, then the oceans will swell and the land will flood and then our homes will be in danger too."

"Sadly, that is very true, but everyone can do something about it," said Uncle Robert. "If everyone made little changes at home and did just a little bit for our planet it could make a big difference. You can save energy by switching a light off in a room when it is not being occupied. Change all of the lightbulbs to low energy ones. People could also switch off their mobile phones, computers, and iPads when they are not using them; all of these small things can be done in the workplace or when out and about, and at home too."

"What do we need to do Uncle Robert?" asked Daisy Dot.

"We need to look after our planet, that is what we need to do," said Uncle Robert.

"Like I said walk, cycle or use public transport.

"We must stop dumping waste and recycle instead.

"And we have to stop polluting our oceans with litter.

"Releasing balloons and lanterns into the atmosphere is a big no-no."

"Yes," said Daisy Dot, "because what goes up must come down, and that is not good for wildlife on land or in the ocean, they often die from eating them."

"Yes, you are so right Daisy Dot," said Uncle Robert.

"We use too much plastic such as straws and bags, these could be changed to paper or reusable ones.

"And remember to switch things off when not in use, and items that use high energy can be replaced with those that use low energy."

Daisy Dot went over to the little stove. Breakfast is finished, we are warm in the sunshine, so I am going to turn the stove off.

From now on Pippi and I will walk to the park and I will walk to school too.

And we will put our reusable waste into recycling bins and find alternatives to plastics.

Pippi barked as though she agreed. She had a dollop of porridge on her nose, she licked it off as she did not want that to go into the waste bin. This made Daisy Dot and Uncle Robert laugh.

"Looks like Pippi has done her bit," said Uncle Robert with a chuckle.

Will you do your bit for the planet too?

How long it takes for some everyday items to decompose...

1, Plastic bottles: 70–400 years
2, Plastic bags: 500–1000 years
3, Fishing line: 600 years
4, Tin can: around 50 years
5, Babies nappies: 500–800 years
6, Glass bottles: 1–2 million years
7, Leather shoes: 25–40 years
8, Aluminium can: 200 years
9, Cigarette: 1–12 years
10, Nylon clothes: 30–40 years

What can you do?...

Reduce plastic use. Look around you, how many plastic items can you see? Count them all.
Think about why you use them, can you reduce the amount you have?
Think about reusing items or items that you can recycle.
Reduce your usage of single-use plastics.

Take part in cleanups and ask your parents and teachers to get involved.
This could be at the beach, the park, or even your local street.

At birthday parties there are often balloons, plastic cups and straws.
Balloons could be replaced with paper kites, paper planes or origami animals.
Plastic table cloths and party bags could be replaced with paper ones.

Decorations could be paper bunting or pom poms.
Will you be kinder to the planet and all who live here?
Stand up for what you stand on: OUR PLANET.
We are the caretakers; we all have to do our bit.
WILL YOU DO YOUR BIT TOO?

Beluga whales like Betsy are in great danger due to many threats from humans.
Plastic pollution, discarded fishing nets and hunting puts them at great risk of becoming endangered.
Beluga whales are highly social animals and they squeal, squeak and chirp, which is why many refer to them as sea canaries.
Their natural habitat is changing due to climate change.
Noise pollution is a big problem; these changes are due to construction projects and oil and gas development.
They suffer from pollution and busy sea vessel traffic.

Orcas (Killer whales) have been known to attack and eat Beluga whales; Beluga whales have been known to swim far into ice-covered waters to avoid being attacked by Orcas, but this can put them at greater risk of attack from polar bears. Unlike Betsy and Chilly in the story, Beluga whales and polar bears are not good friends.
Polar bears will use their powerful strength to pull the Beluga whales onto the ice whenever they find a hole in the ice; which allows them to breathe.
Climate change and pollution are the biggest threats to these beautiful singing canaries of the sea..

Beluga whale Facts

1, They can move their head up and down and side to side, unlike any other whale, because they do not have a fused neck vertebrae.

2, They have bulbous, flexible foreheads called "melons"; this allows them to make facial expressions and sound.

3, Beluga whales can grow up to 16ft long and weigh 3,150lb.

4, When they are born, they are a dark grey and become lighter in colour as they get older, eventually becoming white.

5, Beluga whales are very good divers, they can dive 3,280ft and can stay under water for up to 25 minutes at a time.

Polar bear Facts

1, Polar bears have black skin and although their fur appears white it is actually transparent.

2, Polar bears are the largest carnivores (meat-eaters) that live on land.

3, They can reach speeds of 25mph on land and 10mph in the water.

4, Male polar bears can weigh up to 1500lb.

5, They have an excellent sense of smell; they can detect seals nearly a mile away.

Penguin Facts

1, Penguins can drink seawater.

2, Penguins in Antarctica have no land-based predators.

3, Their black and white plumage is their camouflage; in the water the black plumage on their backs is hard to see from above. The white plumage on their front looks like the sun reflecting off the surface of the water when seen from below.

4, The Emperor penguin is the tallest of the species, reaching 47in in height.

5, Little Blue penguins are the smallest of the species averaging around 13in in height.

Facts on climate change

1, Cows eating habits contribute to greenhouse gasses. Just like us, when cows eat, methane gas builds up in their digestive system and is released in the form of a burp. There are almost 1.5 billion cows releasing all that gas into the atmosphere.

2, Many rain forests are being cut down to make wood and palm oil, and to clear the way for farmland and roads. Our planet needs trees as they act as a filter and absorb carbon dioxide (a greenhouse gas) from the air and then release oxygen back into it.

3, Over the last 150 years, because of human activity, we have been releasing harmful gases into the earth's atmosphere which has caused global temperatures to rise rapidly.

4, A warmer climate causes sea ice to shrink and icebergs to melt, which causes higher sea levels, which can cause floods. This destroys numerous homes of humans and animals.

5, Climate change is already affecting wildlife all around the world. The icy habitats of the polar bears are already melting. Ringed seals make caves in the snow to feed and raise their pups.

6, Orangutans are losing their habitat through forests been cut down and destroyed for palm oil, and to make way for farmland and roads.

7, Many of the nesting beaches where sea turtles lay their eggs are being threatened by rising sea levels.

8, Many sea animals are dying from swallowing tons of plastic and other pollutions and chemicals that are being poured into our oceans.

9, Climate change affects people too, especially people who grow the food we eat every day; the farming communities in developing countries face higher temperatures as well as floods and drought.

10, Climate change affects us all. More rainfall, and changing seasons. Plastic in the seafood you eat.

To save our planet we must all do our bit at home and in school.
Just like Daisy Dot and Pippi, will you do your bit too?

MIRTHQUAKE FOUNDATION

Cetaceans are the Whales, Dolphins and Porpoises. These wondrous mammals have swum our planet's Oceans for some 50 million years. Cetaceans were at home in Planet Water before we renamed it Planet Earth.

Cetaceans have forever sung, and still sing the songs of our Planet Water. They are the wisdom keepers and story tellers.

From a time before memory to this very moment, there has been a profound connection between humans and Cetaceans, a mysterious and much celebrated bond, likely fundamental to our existence.

A global phenomenon of ancient stories, myths and legends relate this remarkable interspecies love affair, a continuous cultural, mystical and spiritual promise since our beginning.

Creation stories of many ancient peoples tell how Humans were once born of Whales or Dolphins. They are the ancestors of our ancestors.

Cetaceans embody our most potent archetypal connection with Nature, our Creator.

- Mirthquake Foundation is dedicated to focusing on creative, cultural and environmental initiatives, emphasising First Nation peoples' current and historical connection with cetaceans.

- Exploring and manifesting the profound and ancient relationship between man and cetaceans, and the role of this relationship in revitalizing and restoring our fractured harmony with nature.

- Improving public awareness of the issues involved in the health of the oceans, environment and associated human issues

The trustees of Mirthquake Foundation are delighted to support Tracey's third book 'Will You Do Your Bit Too?'

In an age where the heartless treatment of animals is so prevalent, strong voices need to be heard to speak for all creatures. The killing, capture and imprisonment of whales and dolphins is perhaps the most powerful testament to our present lack of humanity and severance from Nature, our Creator. We have and continue to perpetrate great cruelty on these remarkable and magnificent beings with whom mankind has had an eternal and profound love affair.

Cetaceans are likely to be vital to our very existence on this water planet and we harm them at our peril.

Tracey's books are essential reading to help children understand everything in this world is interconnected so, our actions are affecting everything around us.

Napier Marten, Founder

Mirthquake Foundation

www.mirthquake.org

A Note from the Author

I first met Napier Marten at a global peaceful demonstration that I had organised to bring media attention to the annual slaughter of dolphins in Taiji, Japan. We met on this very cold day outside the BBC Television centre in London in 2016, and admired each other's work for our finned friends. We both have a passion for cetaceans and believe it is their birthright to swim free in pollution-free oceans and with no harm from humans.

Napier has become a very good friend and we both believe that education is a major part of the key to ending animal suffering, no matter if they live on land or in the sea.

I would like to thank Napier and his Mirthquake Foundation for trusting and believing in me. You have made this book possible.

I hope that children and adults will enjoy this book and learn something from it, and realise we can all unite and protect our planet and all who live here.

We can all do our bit.

An inspired author **Tracey Özdemir**

The talented illustrator Marc Ducrow